LESSONS IN LOVE AND VIOLENCE

Lessons in Love and Violence

Opera in Two Parts

Text for music by
MARTIN CRIMP

Set to music by
GEORGE BENJAMIN

TEXT FOR MUSIC

Text © 2017 by Martin Crimp
Rights administered worldwide by Faber Music Ltd
First published in 2018 by Faber Music Ltd
Bloomsbury House, 74–77 Great Russell Street, London WC1B 3DA
Typeset by Agnesi Text
Printed in England by Caligraving Ltd
All rights reserved

Cover image: Fragments of a horse trapper, 1330–40, England
(*Broderie aux léopards réalisée pour Edouard III d'Angleterre*)
Photo © RMN-Grand Palais (musée de Cluny – musée national du Moyen-Âge)/Franck Raux

ISBN10: 0-571-54055-4
EAN13: 978-0-571-54055-6

Vocal score available on sale:
ISBN10: 0-571-54054-6
EAN13: 978-0-571-54054-9
Full score and orchestral parts available on hire from the publishers

All enquiries relating to *Lessons in Love and Violence* should be addressed to
the Performance Department, Faber Music Ltd
Bloomsbury House, 74–77 Great Russell Street, London WC1B 3DA
Tel: +44 (0) 2079085311   promotion@fabermusic.com

To buy Faber Music publications or to find out about the full range of titles available
please contact your local music retailer or Faber Music sales enquiries:

Faber Music Limited, Burnt Mill, Elizabeth Way, Harlow, Essex, CM20 2HX, England
Tel: +44 (0)1279 82 89 82   Fax: +44 (0)1279 82 89 83
sales@fabermusic.com   fabermusicstore.com

Co-commissioned and co-produced by the Royal Opera
Covent Garden London, Dutch National Opera Amsterdam,
Hamburg State Opera, Opéra de Lyon, Lyric Opera of Chicago,
Gran Teatre del Liceu, Barcelona and Teatro Real Madrid

The first performance was given by The Royal Opera,
Covent Garden, conducted by the composer,
at the Royal Opera House, London, on 10 May 2018

The cast was:

Stéphane Degout (King)
Barbara Hannigan (Isabel)
Gyula Orendt (Gaveston/Stranger)
Peter Hoare (Mortimer)
Samuel Boden (Boy – later Young King)
Jennifer France (Witness 1/Singer 1/Woman 1)
Krisztina Szabó (Witness 2/Singer 2/Woman 2)
Andri Björn Róbertsson (Witness 3/Madman)

Katie Mitchell (stage direction)
Vicki Mortimer (sets and costumes)
James Farncombe (lighting)
Joseph Alford (movement)

Duration of opera: *c.* 100 minutes

CHARACTERS

KING
Baritone

ISABEL, his wife
Soprano

GAVESTON, his advisor and intimate friend / STRANGER
Baritone

MORTIMER, his chief military expert
Tenor

BOY – later YOUNG KING, an adolescent, son of Isabel and King
High Tenor/Haute-contre

WITNESS 1 / SINGER 1 / WOMAN 1
High (Coloratura) Soprano

WITNESS 2 / SINGER 2 / WOMAN 2
Mezzo-soprano

WITNESS 3 / MADMAN
Bass-baritone

Also required (all silent roles):

YOUNG GIRL, daughter of Isabel and King

OTHER WITNESSES / AUDIENCE AT PLAY
to a maximum of, say, twenty

CONTENTS

'Then said Jonathan unto David, whatsoever thy soul desireth,
I will do it even for thee.'

PART ONE

PALACE: *King's Apartments*

KING, MORTIMER, GAVESTON, ISABEL, *the* BOY *and* GIRL.

MORTIMER	It's nothing to do with loving a man. It's love full stop that is poison. The whole human body –
KING	Yes – we hear you – love full stop –
MORTIMER	And the money –
KING	Always the money – always the human body –
MORTIMER	– the money you spend –
KING	– we will spend whatever we like –
MORTIMER	The money you spend with Gaveston while people starve is unacceptable –
KING	– Ah – ah – 'with Gaveston' – 'unacceptable' –
MORTIMER	– yes when the price of bread –
KING	Don't bore me with the price of bread. Don't block my mind with politics.
MORTIMER	You are the king.
KING	Then treat me – Mortimer – as king. Love me. Defer to me. Defer to my friend and advisor Gaveston. Let us spend money on poetry and music. Or would you rather we preferred for our entertainment

I

	human blood and the machinery of killing?
MORTIMER	No one is talking about blood.
KING	Oh? What? No one? –
MORTIMER	Nor do I fight wars for my entertainment –
KING	– Who is no one? Am I no one? –
MORTIMER	– I fight to protect our people –
KING	– I thought I was king. Who am I, Gaveston? – tell me.
GAVESTON	King – you are king.
KING	King – I am king. Don't call me no one, Mortimer. Don't go out into the world and call love poison. Love makes us human.
MORTIMER	So does the need to kill. So – forgive me – does politics.
KING	Do you want – Mortimer – to be me? –
MORTIMER	I don't understand.
KING	– want to be me – – take my wife – Mortimer – – use my bed – Mortimer – – murder and kill and take my crown? Because cities will burn and wherever you touch the immaculate surface of her skin your politics will leave streaks of my blood. But maybe – tell me – does Mortimer keep a cat?

Takes GIRL *on his lap.*

They say there's an insane person claiming
    to be king
on evidence provided by his cat.
Maybe his name is Mortimer.

MORTIMER   I am loyal.

KING   What did he say?

GAVESTON   He said he is loyal.
He claims not to have
a cat.

KING   He tells me my people are starving – but who
have I ever harmed?

ISABEL   No one. Yourself – sometimes.

KING   Not you?

ISABEL   Never.

KING   You see: I am entirely innocent.
And have I hurt Gaveston?

ISABEL   Ask Gaveston.

KING   Have I hurt you, Gaveston?

GAVESTON *turns away.*

I ASKED YOU A QUESTION ANSWER ME.

GAVESTON   Not when you grip my neck.
Not when you hold my right hand deliberately
    over a flame.
Not even when you have forced me to swim
    in winter under the dull grey ice
    till my lungs are beginning to split –

Oh but when you let that man
equate money with love and the whole
    human body
with shame and bitterness –
when he questions your right to be king –
when his eyes move – look – like a sly animal's
    over everything you own
then I want to run at his throat with a steel razor –
Take his property.

MORTIMER   No – none of this is true.

GAVESTON   Take Mortimer's property.
Take his house – take over his land. Punish him.
Give me his rents.
Remove from his finger that fat gold ring.

MORTIMER   None of this is true.

ISABEL   But Mortimer is our friend –

KING   Yes Mortimer is our friend –

GAVESTON   Mortimer – Mortimer – even the name
    means death –

KING   Mortimer is our friend
and is loyal and in his own cold way – believe me –
Mortimer loves each one of us.

GAVESTON   Then why in his own cold way when I take
    my hand
and I place it here –
place it like this –

He takes the KING *by the throat perhaps – a gesture that suggests both violence and intimacy.*

4

	– does he feel
	– look at his face –
	disgust?
	Tell me I'm wrong – dead man Mortimer.
ISABEL	Tell him he's wrong.

MORTIMER *looks away.*

KING	Oh my poor friend Mortimer –
	from this moment you have no land –
	from today you will have no property.
	The clothes you are wearing
	you no longer own.
	And being now nothing
	you have no name.

ISABEL	Don't call him nothing.

KING	I say that he has no name:
	do not contradict me, Isabel.
	I say he is nothing.
	I say that all I can see where Mortimer
	once stood
	is the black space of a collapsing star.

GAVESTON	But I see the ring.

KING	(*to* BOY) Ah. Sweetheart.

BOY	What is it
	daddy?

KING	Bring Gaveston the ring.

MORTIMER *is impassive. The* BOY *struggles to remove the ring.*

GAVESTON	The boy needs a knife.

ISABEL   No!

KING   No violence please.
              Let ours be a regiment
              of tolerance and love.

                         SCENE 2

PALACE: *Isabel's Apartments, some months later*
ISABEL, MORTIMER, *the* BOY *and* GIRL, *and a number of* WITNESSES.

ISABEL   Who are these people, Mortimer?
              They're frightening my children.

MORTIMER   I've travelled, Isabel.
              I wanted to see my country.
              I began in the mountains
              but there was nothing to eat but stone.
              So I came down to the spring meadow
              but in each refuge
              I found a shepherd with his throat cut
              and the clean bones of animals.
              In the foothills
              I dug for roots
              and lay for heat
              in the ash of burnt villages – but –
              closer – Isabel – to our own city
              I found these witnesses.
              And led them in secret
              here – Isabel – to your door.

ISABEL   Why?

MORTIMER   Listen.

ISABEL	What is it she's holding?
WITNESS 2	My husband died – forgive me – in your husband's war – but then your husband gave our land – he gave away our home – he gave our property – to Gaveston. I came here with nothing but my body and sold it over and over – forgive me. I had a baby – oh forgive me – but my baby died and this is my baby's ash. Since Gaveston has taken everything then I would like him to take my baby too. Yes – yes – here is my baby too. Take it.
ISABEL	Keep her away – I am not Gaveston. My name's not Gaveston – keep her away from me.
WITNESS 1	They say one jewel from Gaveston's silver cup – one cut emerald – could've fed my whole dead family –
WITNESS 2	They say he's magic and can predict the future. I hope his future is to be burned alive.
WITNESS 1	They say one night of the music for that man Gaveston –
ISABEL	'They say' – 'they say' – that's not a witness –
WITNESS 1	– say just one night costs the same as one whole year of our labour –
ISABEL	No there is no connection –

WITNESS 1	– one whole year of work –
ISABEL	– no connection between our music and your labour.
MORTIMER	Tell her what else the people say.
WITNESS 3	They say we know why the poor sleep three in a bed but why do the rich?
ISABEL	(*to* GIRL) Bring me a cup of vinegar.

Pause

> Listen – witnesses – I respect each one of you.
> I am a human being and a mother too.
> My body is forked like yours:
> it loves – and breaks –
> like a common criminal's –
> with the same pain.
> But do not come here
> trying to put a price on music.

She takes the cup of vinegar from the GIRL.

> This – is acid –
> and this pearl . . .

She takes a pearl from around her neck.

> . . . this pearl – you are right –
> would buy each one of you a house with
> fourteen rooms

and beds and winter firewood but –
the beauty of the pearl
is not what the pearl can buy.
The beauty of the pearl – like the slow radiance
    of music –
is what the pearl is.
Look.

She drops the pearl into the vinegar.

Fourteen rooms dissolve.
And the whole winter stock of wood.
The dull dreams of the average dreamer
– money – property – burn away
in the acid of   of   of
of pure and inexchangeable value.
And? – what? – which one of you will drink it?
Maybe this one – this one – you – you –
    three in a bed – the slanderer!

She tries to force WITNESS 3 *to drink.*
MORTIMER *grabs her and knocks away the cup.*

Now give them all money and get them all out.

The WITNESSES *go.*

BOY   Why do the poor sleep
                three in a bed – mummy?

ISABEL   To keep warm – sweetheart.

BOY   And why – mummy – do the rich?

ISABEL   The man told a lie – sweetheart.

BOY	Why did the man tell a lie?
	Why did the man tell a lie – mummy?
ISABEL	Because he is poor and angry.
	Mortimer – tell me – what is it like to kill?
MORTIMER	There is an art to killing – but no joy.
ISABEL	What is it I should do?
MORTIMER	Provide an entertainment.
	Empty Gaveston's mind with music –
	and I can destroy him.
ISABEL	No one must harm my husband.
MORTIMER	No one will harm your husband –
	only Gaveston.
	What are you thinking, Isabel?
ISABEL	Move away.
	The children are watching us.

SCENE 3

PALACE: *A Theatre*
*The theatre's curtain is closed – empty chairs are set out for
an audience.*
KING *and* GAVESTON.
Later, ISABEL, *the* CHILDREN, SINGERS 1+2, MORTIMER.
KING *seizes* GAVESTON *by the wrist.*

KING	How can I love you?
	A man with the steel hand
	and sleepy smile of an assassin.

GAVESTON   Yes I'm a human razor:
             take care or I'll cut your throat.

KING   You bite your fingernails like a boy does –
             the skin's broken where you punched the wall –
             why did you punch the wall?

GAVESTON   Love is a prison:
             I wanted to see daylight.

KING   How can I love a man who calls love a prison? –
             who says he would cut my throat?
             How would you kill me, Gaveston? –
             would it be slow? –
             or sudden?

GAVESTON   I'd only kill you for money.

KING   For money? – kill me for money? –
                  how much money?

GAVESTON   How much would you pay me?

KING   How long will it take to die? – I'll pay you for
                  every minute.
             Tell me my future, Gaveston.

GAVESTON   Then open your hand.

KING *opens his hand.*

KING   What can you see?

Pause

GAVESTON   Here – look – is my baby king.
             He appoints ministers and sets villages alight
             even in his painted cradle –

and his rattle is a box of emeralds.
And here –
        – keep it still –
                – is his child bride Isabel.
This same hand that now seals the instruction
to sever a man's head
strips bare her silk body.
Now your belovèd boy's torn out of her –
and another child –
and this – look – shows how the children grow –
so fast does life move till already this line cutting
        across
means war or fire or storm or crops burning –

KING   Yes yes politics – but where –

GAVESTON   – means Mortimer testing for Isabel
                the machinery of killing –

KING   – Mortimer – machinery –
                but where is my future? –
                where is my brother Gaveston?

GAVESTON   You know where I am:
                inside your life.
                I've no life out of it.
                I live where you are looking:
                in the hard palm of your hand.

ISABEL *enters with the* TWO CHILDREN.
Behind them, the AUDIENCE *for the performance, who come*
and sit in the chairs.

ISABEL   Please everyone – be seated.

GAVESTON   What is the music, Isabel?

ISABEL   The killing of Saul
                and of Jonathan his son.

GAVESTON   I don't like killing – neither will your children.

ISABEL   A child knows it's normal to kill our enemies –
                but this will be David's lament: there is no
                        violence.

KING has taken his place in front row of audience,
with his CHILDREN beside him.

GAVESTON   I have no enemies.

ISABEL   Please – sit next to me.

GAVESTON   Won't you sit with your husband.

ISABEL   I am closer to my husband
                Gaveston
                the closer I am to you.

As they sit together in the back row of the audience,
the onstage curtain goes up to reveal TWO FEMALE SINGERS,
exquisitely dressed.

SINGERS   *And David said:*
                where is my brother?
                where is my brother Jonathan?
                'They fastened his body'
                – said the messenger –
                'to the wall of Beth-shan.'
                Where is my brother?
                where is my brother Jonathan?

GAVESTON   Oh how very beautifully they sing –

ISABEL   You have tears in your eyes –

SINGERS	*'They took down his body to be burned.'*
ISABEL	– is it too tight?
GAVESTON	Is what?
ISABEL	The ring, the ring – is Mortimer's ring too tight for your finger? Don't move away from me – no – sit close sit close to me Gaveston sit closer –
SINGERS	*And David said:* *where is my brother?* *oh where is my brother Jonathan?*

But GAVESTON *stands when he sees* MORTIMER *staring at him from the edge of the space. Members of the onstage* AUDIENCE *stand around him as if to block an escape. The* SINGERS *continue.*

GAVESTON	Dead man Mortimer – what've you come to tell me, dead man Mortimer? – the price of butter? – or is it the price of bread?
MORTIMER	I've come for my property.
GAVESTON	Oh? Oh? Property? Here's your property. Take her.

He pushes ISABEL *towards* MORTIMER.
Now the KING *notices the disturbance.*

SINGERS	*'Where is my brother Jonathan?'*
KING	Arrest this man. Stop the song. Stop the music. I SAID STOP THE MUSIC NOW!

The onstage SINGERS *stop.*

I order the arrest of Mortimer.

No one moves.

I command you to listen to your king.

No one moves.

I command you to kneel down at my feet
and swear to me your obedience.

No one moves.

NO BUT YOU WILL SPARE ME GAVESTON.

SCENE 4

*PALACE: Private Apartment
The* KING *alone, holding a letter.*
ISABEL *enters.*

ISABEL	I'm cold. I was dreaming. Come and sleep.
KING	I never sleep.
ISABEL	I'm cold. Come and hold me.
KING	(*reads*) 'And one man drove a sword through his body and another beheaded him in a ditch.'
ISABEL	You're tired: come and sleep.
KING	I couldn't save him. I couldn't save him, Isabel.

15

ISABEL	Stop now. Come and sleep.
KING	Who have I ever harmed?
ISABEL	I'm cold. Even my lips are cold. Why are my lips so cold? Won't you kiss me?
KING	I could hold his hand – like this – steady like this – Isabel – over a flame and he would meet my eyes while his hand burned and burned over that same flame and smile.
ISABEL	Ah.

ISABEL *turns away from him.*

	Why should you love him – tell me – still love him – tell me – whom all the world hates?
KING	Because he loved me more than all the world. But why have you turned away?
ISABEL	Turned away?
KING	Turned to the dark – yes – turned away from me.
ISABEL	How have I turned to the dark?
KING	To hide your face there in the dark.
ISABEL	I haven't turned to the dark.
KING	Then show me your face.
ISABEL	No.

KING	Show me your eyes.
ISABEL	No.
KING	Isabel!

She turns back to him.

ISABEL	Here is my face.
	And here – look – are my tears.
	What have I ever hidden?
	No part of this body.
	No part of my mind – not my opinions.
	Not ever my love.
	I'm not the one my poor poor sweetheart
	who has turned and turned
	and keeps on deliberately turning to the dark.

KING	I will break him.
	I will break Mortimer open.
	I will cut his living body into four –

ISABEL	I am taking our son –

KING	– will hunt out each associate of his crime –

ISABEL	I am taking our son –

KING	– smoke them out of their own homes –
	– drown whole cities in their blood –

ISABEL	I said I am taking our son to Mortimer.
	Only he can protect him. (*Pause*) Don't you see?

No reaction from the KING.

Then stay in the dark.
Play king alone here in the dark.

We will leave you the box of toys.

She goes.
After a long pause, KING *goes back to the letter.*

KING   (*reads*) 'but he mocked them
              and asked by whose authority he should die.
              They said: that of Mortimer.
              And Gaveston replied:
              Mortimer is a dog.
              His snout is between the queen's legs
              and his breath smells of murder.
              So they bound his hands.
              And one man drove a sword through his body
              and . . .
              and another . . .'

PART TWO

SCENE 5

MORTIMER'S HOUSE
MORTIMER, ISABEL and BOY. Later, the MADMAN.
The GIRL is skipping.

MORTIMER	D'you like dogs? I'll buy you a dog. Or maybe you'd like a lion? Would you like to be king and keep lions?
BOY	My father is king
MORTIMER	Your father cannot be king – he wants you to take his place.
BOY	I'm a boy. I have no experience.
MORTIMER	Your mother and I will advise you.
BOY	What kind of dog?
ISABEL	A greyhound –
MORTIMER	– yes an immaculate greyhound. But first you must show us you understand justice and can protect the people.
BOY	Oh?

MORTIMER	Yes from decadence and terror.
	Let the man in.

MADMAN *comes in.*

	This man is promoting revolution.
	He claims to be king.
MADMAN	No not a claim but a totally true statement.
ISABEL	Tell my son what it is you believe.
MADMAN	I believe I am king and demand to be heard.
MORTIMER	Oh he demands. Test him.
BOY	What is your evidence?
MADMAN	I am told I am king not only by inheritance but by the will of the universe encoded in a bright pattern of stars.
MORTIMER	Test him. Who told him?
BOY	Who told you
	you are king?
MADMAN	I was told by Felicity.
BOY	Who is Felicity?
MADMAN	Felicity has green eyes. Felicity is a cat.
MORTIMER	Test him. I said you must test him.
BOY	My father is king.
	And I will be king after him.
	To claim to be king is – oh – don't you see? – unintelligent.

MORTIMER	No – is a crime. Say it.
BOY	Is a crime.
MADMAN	No not a crime but a totally true statement.
MORTIMER	And to make this claim is to ask to be put to death. Say it.
BOY	But his mind's not right.
MORTIMER	Say it –
ISABEL	– we need you to say it.
MADMAN	No I am of totally sound mind and I will destroy this child and rule with my cat in perpetual glory.
ISABEL	He says he'll destroy you.
BOY	But his mind's not right. Mortimer – spare him.
MADMAN	I don't ask to be spared I ask you to offer me respect and obedience.
MORTIMER	(*taking the* GIRL'*s skipping rope*) We can offer you this rope.
BOY	No!
MADMAN	No not rope but respect and –
BOY	Be merciful!

MORTIMER *begins to strangle the* MADMAN *with the skipping rope.*

MORTIMER	Let one poisonous idea leak out into the world and the whole world will be contaminated. Look. I said look at this clearly and learn.

BOY *tries to bury his face in* ISABEL *but* ISABEL *– although disturbed – forces him to look.*

> Understand –
> that when you are king –
> there will be no room for one man's love
>   for another –
> no room for madness –
> or for disorder inside –
> the machinery of the regulated world.

MADMAN *dies.*

BOY   Ah.
                 But mercy . . .

MORTIMER   When a man will be cut into pieces and burned
                 a rope is mercy.

BOY   What kind of crown
                 will I have?

MORTIMER   Your father's true crown of gold.

BOY   Where is my father? –

MORTIMER   Your father is safe.

BOY   – is he in prison?

ISABEL   Take your sister into the garden please
                 and pick her a sweet apple.

The CHILDREN *go out.*

                 Tell me: how will you take the crown?

MORTIMER   In front of witnesses. By logical argument.

ISABEL	And after that? I said: and after that? What are you, Mortimer?
MORTIMER	I am a man.
ISABEL	Then touch me.

SCENE 6

PRISON
KING, MORTIMER, WITNESSES.
Later, the STRANGER.

KING	Drumming – I can hear drumming. What is it you want from me?
MORTIMER	The crown.
KING	Drumming – I can hear drumming.
MORTIMER	Give me the crown and your son will be king.
KING	Drumming – I can hear drumming.
MORTIMER	Your son has been chosen king –
KING	(*mocking*) *My son has been chosen* –
MORTIMER	He needs the crown.
KING	– *and needs the crown.* Then show me my son. Let me speak to my children! Drumming – I can hear drumming.
MORTIMER	(*to* WITNESSES) Write this down:

he is unfit to rule.
Write he imagines drumming.

KING   Oh – I am a bad person.
Oh I have turned to the dark –
And the man I chose as brother –
I could not save –
write that I could not save him –

MORTIMER   Self-pity. Write nothing. The crown.

KING   Yes I have let my own people starve –
have wept to exquisite music –

MORTIMER   The crown –

KING   – while the hay lay drowned.

MORTIMER   – in front of these witnesses – the crown –

KING   Yes I have broken my own country's back
but I will
never never
let you
dead man Mortimer
take this crown.

KING *seizes* MORTIMER's *wrist.*

What's your opinion now
of the human body?
You and my wife –
are you a good fit?
When your tongue's inside her
– Mortimer –
can you still taste the husband?

24

MORTIMER *frees himself.*

MORTIMER   Write – write this down –
            that lechery –
            that sodomy –
            have decayed his mind.
            That he degrades his own wife –
            betrays his own son –
            so the crown will pass out of his family
            and never return.
            Write what he said.
            Write he is no one.

KING   I am not no one.

MORTIMER   Write that instead of a man this man has chosen
            to be nothing.

MORTIMER *makes to go.*

KING   Take it.
            Take it, Mortimer – and commend me to my son.

MORTIMER *takes the crown and leaves with* WITNESSES.
TWO WOMEN *remain.*
Pause

            What do you want from me?

WOMEN 1+2   There is a man waiting.

KING   What man?

WOMEN 1+2   He comes from Mortimer.
            He brings you light.

KING   Brings me what light?

WOMEN 1+2   What shall we say to him?

KING   Say to come in.

STRANGER *appears.*

WOMEN 1+2   This is the man.

KING   Come forward into the light.
I know you've come to murder me.
Tell me your name.

STRANGER   I am a person all the world hates.
I stand outside every door:
no one invites me in.
When pear-blossom opens in spring
I nod to the drum –
hum to the wooden flute:
but no one invites me to dance.

KING   Come forward into the light.

STRANGER   Like you I'm king of a stone palace –

KING   Tell me your name.

STRANGER   – and like you I am always alone.
You know my name.

STRANGER *steps into the light.*

KING   (*without expression*) Gaveston –

STRANGER   My name is not Gaveston –

KING   I know you've been sent to murder me –

STRANGER   My name is not Gaveston –

KING   – will it be slow? – or sudden? –

STRANGER   – you know my name.

KING   Tell me my future –

STRANGER   You know what my name is –

KING   – how will I die? –

STRANGER   – open your hand.

STRANGER takes the KING's hand.

Pause

Here – look – is the living king.
Naked in his cradle
he rattles the wood frame
and the world – oh the world comes running.
See how the whole line of his life
is tense with pleasure
as Fate unwinds from its oiled machine
one long silk thread –

KING   But how will I die?

STRANGER   – until here – look – the machinery spits blood –

KING   I said how will I die?

STRANGER   His wife cries out in the night for Mortimer.

KING   I said tell me – tell me –

STRANGER   His own child staggers up onto the throne now
as puppet-king and takes his own place
on the puppet-stage of History.

KING   – how am I going to die?

STRANGER   How?

Don't you see:
The thread is already broken.
You are already dead.

KING   No.

Long pause

Why do I feel nothing?

STRANGER   The dead
can't feel.

KING   No.
Why is my mind blank?

STRANGER   The dead
have no thoughts.

KING   No. When
did I die?

STRANGER   When
means nothing.

KING   And how?
Was it murder?

STRANGER   Murder – murder
means nothing.

KING   No.
Make me feel.

STRANGER   I can't.

KING   No.
Make me alive again.

STRANGER   I can't.

KING   Hold my body over the fire
             Gaveston.
             Make me alive.

STRANGER   My name
             is not Gaveston.

KING   Bind me to a metal rack.
             Burn me.
             Make me alive.

STRANGER   The dead
             cannot burn.

KING   Love me.
             Burn me.
             Make me alive.

STRANGER   The dead
             cannot love.

KING   Love me.
             Bind me to a rack of hot metal.
             Hold me – burn me forever
             in a crucible of fire.

PALACE: *A Theatre*
The theatre as before, its curtain closed, and rows
of empty chairs.
ISABEL *and the* BOY – *who is now the* YOUNG KING –
both in mourning.
Later, the AUDIENCE.

ISABEL   What is the music?

YOUNG KING   I have forbidden music.

ISABEL   Then what is behind the curtain?

YOUNG KING   It is
                an entertainment.

ISABEL   Ah.

Pause

                Who will be invited
                to the entertainment?

YOUNG KING   Yes.
                Who shall we invite?
                My father?

ISABEL   Don't play.

YOUNG KING   This is not play.

ISABEL   You're a child.

YOUNG KING   No I am king.

ISABEL   What is behind the curtain?

YOUNG KING	What do you want mummy to be behind the curtain?
ISABEL	Oh – a low summer moon. Your father – my innocence.
YOUNG KING	My father's dead. On no side of this curtain mummy are we innocent.

Short pause

	Let me explain to you the entertainment. In a deep pit under the earth a man and a woman murder a king. On the vacant throne to gratify the people they install the woman's child and plan to conceal the murder –
ISABEL	No – where is Mortimer?
YOUNG KING	– but from under the earth echoes out the king his father's agony. The child learns –
ISABEL	– I said to you where is Mortimer? –
YOUNG KING	– and offers dead man Mortimer no mercy.

An AUDIENCE files on silently to sit facing the closed curtain.

> The name of his crime
> mummy
> is cut
> into his body –

ISABEL   No – stop – spare him –

YOUNG KING   – and – when he has read its name –
                        mummy –

ISABEL   – no – spare him –

YOUNG KING   – we cut out his eyes.

The onstage AUDIENCE have settled into their seats.

> With a scene then of a human being
> broken and broken
> by the rational application
> of human justice
> our entertainment begins.